You Want It, Don't You, Billy?

Published by Reed Independent, Australia.

Printed by KDP.

Available from Australianplays.org, Amazon.com, Kindle and Smashwords estores and most major book retail chains and online retail outlets worldwide as:
paperback: ISBN 9780994630148
ebook: ISBN 9780994630155

A catalogue record of this book is available from the National Library of Australia

YOU WANT IT, DON'T YOU, BILLY?

a play

BILL REED

R

Also by Bill Reed

Plays
Burke's Company
Bullsh/ More Bullsh
Cass Butcher Bunting
Mr Siggie Morrison with his Comb and Paper
Truganinni
Living in Black Holes (anthology)
Living on Mars (anthology)
Living on Mars: the play
Daddy the 8th
Truganinni Inside Out
Auntie and the Girl
Mirror, Mirror
Little She
You Want It, Don't You, Billy?
The Pecking Order
Jack Charles is Up and Fighting
Just Out of Your Ground
I Don't Know What to Do with You!
Paddlesteamer

novels
The Pipwink Papers\
Me, the Old Man
Stigmata
Ihe
Dogod
Crooks
Tusk
Throw her back
Are You Human?
Tasker Tusker Tasker
Awash
1001 Lankan Nights book 1
1001 Lankan Nights book 2
Passing Strange

Nonfiction
Water Workout

Award-winning short stories (see also title 'Passing Strange')
Messman on the C.E. Altar
The 200-year Old Feet
The Case Inside
Blind Freddie Among the Pickle Jars
The Old Ex-serviceman
The Shades of You my Dandenong

'By this time I have ready your next play, YOU WANT IT, DON'T YOU, BILLY? No one else has read it here yet, but you might be interested to hear that the sense of evil it generated shook me so much that I spent the night in a sleeping bag at the foot of my daughter's bed (she wouldn't let me in!) because my husband was away and I was scared.'

Carmel Dunn
(then) Director, Play Reading Service
Melbourne Theatre Company

The Premieres

Premiered by the Nimrod Theatre, Sydney, 9 May 1975.
Director: John Bell
Cast: Robyn Nevin/ John Gaden/ Maurice Tarragano/ Christy Hak
Designer: Kim Carpenter
Lighting: Simon Jenkins

Also premiered in Melbourne by the Melbourne Theatre Company on the same night.

The Characters

BILLY 40-year-old husband. The engineer, slide-ruled, but not recognizing the correct result like he used to

BILLY his wife. The shock-therapy disclosures

TIM 21-year-old 'weekend' neighbour. All those weekends waiting to be called...

Act 1
1.

(The bedroom of a weekend cottage in a suburbanised rural area.

Setting is with moonlight outside. The moonlight floods the room whenever the lights are off.

The reading lamp is on over the double bed in which are BILL and BILLY. He is lying with his back to her, pretending to be asleep. She is sitting up and has a book open on her lap but she is not reading, only staring straight ahead.

She exudes lethargy; her only movement is to sigh deeply but this is not done emotionally but more to seemingly expunge the energy from her body.

Sound over is that of a tape recorder in the other room. Berlioz. It is loud and invading but neither of them seem to care. It is just 'out there'.

After a while she turns and looks at his sleeping form. She does this for a long time, as though she has to gather momentum to speak. When she manages to do so it is in monotone.)

BILLY: Why pretend?

BILL: What?

BILLY: To be asleep. That's what women are supposed to do.

(Pause)

BILL: Nup.

BILLY: (sighs) You are.

BILL: I'm trying to force myself to sleep.

BILLY: Where are we?

>*(He turns to look at her, scrutinizes her face. She meekly looks back down at him bluntly.*

BILL: All right?

BILLY: Where is our buzz in all the atoms?

BILL: You're kidding.

BILLY: No, everything's whirling. Don't you find it strange we are still here kinda fixed, in forms, not going, you know, whirl-whirl? Unchanged. No going-to. No coming-from. Stuck stasis, sort of thing.

BILL: Get some sleep.

BILLY: Does that help?

BILL: *Try.*

BILLY: Oh?

BILL: I'm getting tired of all this, Billy.

BILLY: Of course you are.

BILL: Hey, don't come at that. I am. What am I supposed to do? Put you to sleep now?

BILLY: I shamed you, did I?

BILL: Oh, cock.

BILLY: I didn't mean to shame you. I just fell ill.

BILL: (exasperated) It was weeks ago, okay?

BILLY: You've hardly spoken to me since weeks ago.

BILL: I've spoken, I've spoken.

(Pause)

BILLY: (again) I just fell ill.

BILL: Shit. Listen to your music. It's your music. You won't listen to it. I can't help listening to it. That's why I can't get to sleep.

(He rolls over.

She continues to look down at him and he can feel her unblinking eyes on him, until he finally overreacts out of annoyance.)

BILL: What the hell are you looking at now?

(But she remains looking at him nonetheless – perhaps not really seeing him; perhaps pretending that she's not really seeing him. It gives, though, a clear indication that she can no longer absorb what he thinks about what she's doing. Other than that, there is no malice nor rudeness in it. Just looking.

Again he covers himself up from her. But he is obviously still on the alert.)

BILLY: I'll read.

BILL: That's the ticket. You read.

(But she makes no movement to pick up the book. To make matters worse for his sleeping, the disc jams in the middle of a track... and almost simultaneously her reading lamp goes out.

The bedroom is plunged into moonlight.

NOTE: This is the crisp, shadowish lighting atmosphere of much of what follows.

Both have stiffened. She gropes for him, manages:)

BILLY: What?

BILL: Ssh!

(There are a few scratching, then relative silence)

BILLY: *(again)* What? Bill!

BILL: Power breakdown or something.

BILLY: *(with odd surety)* No.

BILL: *(sharply)* What do you mean?

BILLY: I know it's not that.

BILL: How do you know?

BILLY: *(evasively)* A power breakdown?
   (laughs bitterly, taps her own head)
Yeah. In here.

BILL: Good Christ. The power's gone, that's all.

(But he still doesn't move to go and investigate. For a moment it looks as if he might do so, but then he turns over

11

again.

BILLY remains sitting up, listening. Then hears movement down the passage. She grabs hold of him, motions. He sits up and listens.

Whatever it was has stopped. He scornfully shrugs off her hand, lies back down.

Yet he keeps his eye on her. And almost inevitably the noise starts up again and its scratching gets closer. She clutches at him; he shrugs her off once more.

What she is hearing mounts in sound all around her. It reaches fantasy levels in her mind and assume the stage. The terror she starts to feel is reflected in her absolute rigidity, until...

Framed in the doorway by the moonlight is a figure in overcoat and hat pulled down. She struggles to overcome her fright, then sobs aloud.

BILL sits bolt upright, but the figure vanishes from the doorway.

Blackout)

2.

(BILLY is sitting alone in the bed. She is not panicked any longer but sits propped up by pillows and very comfortably.

BILL comes back in, stands looking at her)

BILLY: (monotone)   I saw him.

BILL: Sure you did.

BILLY: I saw him.

BILL: Billy, the power's off everywhere. It' s a break somewhere.

BILLY: I did, you know.

BILL: You had to go and talk to that nutty old bag at the shop about that intruder around here lately. You just let her go on and on.

BILLY: (*still flatly*) I saw him.

BILL: You saw what she put in your mind. Why'd you want to come down here this weekend?

BILLY: Not because of that.

BILL: Why would it be because of that?

BILLY: I just said it wasn't.

BILL: And that's…
   (waves at doorway)
just coincidence?

BILLY: (ignoring him) It's been so many weeks. So much city, wasn't it? Punctures. That's what I felt like.

   (Pause)

BILL: Yeah, I know, love.

   (He climbs back into bed. But this time he keeps a sharp eye out on the door. Finally:)

BILLY: I'm not seeing things. Still

BILL: Hey, it'll take time. What he told you… it'll take lots of time probably. Best thing is to get your head down, try to sleep it off.

BILLY: You don't believe anything I say anymore?

BILL: (strained) Fair go.

BILLY: I saw him.

BILL: Yeah, well, he's gone now.

BILLY: (factually) I can still hear him outside.
    (to his sigh of impatience)
I really can. Scratching. Humming. Wires.
    (then blandly)
What's wrong with me. *Really*.

BILL: (harshly) Don't you know?

BILLY: Do you?

BILL: The truth?

BILLY: Yes, yes.

BILL: The truth is I'm tired of guessing, I guess.

BILLY: (monotone again) Our earths. Are you still sure you know your way around our mine?
    (pause)
That you're tired of guessing anymore.
    (and)
I might have been born right here. How the particles are never still, always in a different place. At the same time. Here, there.
    (bitter laugh)
Born in out nutshell.
    (and)
You really ought to stop guessing, you know. There really might have been someone there. On my earths.

14

(BILL snorts derision, turns away. She continues to look down at him nonetheless.

Scratching and breathing unpleasantly crowd in upon her again. These rise to a new peak, when, very timely, the reading lamp and the music comes back on.

For a moment she can sigh with relief until, a moment later, they switch off again. But before she can react badly once more, the power returns)

BILL: There. *That's* a power breakdown.

BILLY: I think you ought to phone.

BILL: Billy, give it a rest.

BILLY: I really do think you ought to phone for somebody.

BILL: Shit.

(He switches out the reading lamp. The room is moonlit once more and she remains sitting up.

Something moves by the window. She looks over. The same figure is framed in the window, outside. She cries out. BILL looks up, sees the figure before it slides away)

BILL: *Jesus!*

(He manages to force himself to get out of bed and throw open the window, then look out)

BILLY: (whine) Phone, Bill.

(Somewhat recovered, he hurries out of the bedroom. He is heard making a phone call and then obviously finishes it. A brief pause before he looks back in)

BILL: Try that light.

(She switches on the reading lamp but the power is still off)

BILL: The power's on down the road. It's us. It's got to be him.

BILLY: Come back in!

BILL: (meaning his mobile) It's flat. Where's yours?

BILLY: I didn't bring it!

BILL: I'll try getting the power back on, phone. Don't make it worse. I'll get the power on, or get over to next door.

BILLY: Don't leave me!

BILL: Just stay put.
  (stops)
Unless you know what's going on out there…

BILLY: (ignoring that) Please don't leave me!

BILL: All you have to do is shout.

BILLY: I am!

(He ignores her plea and withdraws. She listens desperately but soon there is silence. Nothing is moving and she feels it

BILLY: Bill?

(But no response. She sits terribly alone.

The scratching, murmuring starts up again and mounts to consume her.

When it reaches an intolerable level, suddenly there is a shout, then sounds of a short and vicious fight outside.

Then a silence again. Very still.

She forces herself out of bed, but breathless cannot move far from it.

She cringes back onto the bed when someone moves, deliberately, inside the house. The person's breathing looms, overwhelms her. No scream will come.

The INTRUDER's silhouette comes to be framed in the doorway. He stands there looking at her, listening to her shallow breathing.

Blackout)

3.

(Instantaneous lighting back on.

The INTRUDER has not moved. His teeth shine in the moonlight as he slowly grins at her. When he speaks his voice is unnatural and contrived yet menacing real)

INTRUDER: You scream.

(She clamps her hand over her mouth, preventing herself from doing so. And when he moves closer, she begins shaking so much that he stops)

INTRUDER: Changed my mind. You scream and he gets hurt real bad.

BILLY: No. Please.

INTRUDER: Get over to the window.

17

BILLY: Please.

INTRUDER: Now, why don't you go over to the window?

(Mesmerically she does as he commands. She stands outlined at the window by the moonlight. Her night dress is translucent)

INTRUDER: Open your legs.
 (she can't)
Now, why won't you open your legs?
 (she does so finally)
There. Have they got varicose veins on the up? I'm going to find that out, aren't I? Real close inspection. Lumps. I really like them lumpy. Funny, never been funny. They look alright, yours. Why aren't you opening them a bit more? Like waiting for the world's biggest.
 (she is sobbing now)
Now rub yourself.
 (she can only shake her head)
Just up and down your legs, what's wrong with that? Why aren't you rubbing yourself up and down your legs?
 (she tries to get away with the outside of her legs)
The insides. Thighs. And where they go to. Why aren't you doing that?
 (she can barely do so, yet his voice gets husky)
Turn around now.
 (she shakes her head)
I think you ought to turn around.
 (she does so fearfully)
Open the window. Pussy, pussy. You can look out. Why aren't you looking out?

(BILLY looks out of the window and then down, has difficulty divining what she is looking at.

There is a moan from outside.

Before she can react, the INTRUDER has crossed to her, has her held from behind. He has her held rigidly against

18

*him, his hands on her breasts. He breaths into her ears, first
one then the other. Then whispers coarsely to her)*

INTRUDER: Scream? Why would you want to scream if I'm
around? Tucking you in, all safe and sound. You want it too,
don't you, Billy?

> *(She shakes her head, but he begins to hurt her until she
> nods savagely)*

INTRUDER: Sure, I know how much you want it. Aren't you
nice, like. Bed still steaming off you. And...
(he whispers something in her ear again; she can't escape)
Why didn't you say how you saw how I tie them up? Would you
like me to tie you up like that? Nicer. Nicer?
(laughs)
Scream? You? No, if you'd looked proper, you'da seen how I
can just pull on that rope around the dope's neck. Right? *Right?*
Sure it's right. I'm always right. I'm the one pulling the strings,
ha ha. It's quite a go when they scream sometimes. We can try it
out. You scream, go ahead. Scream 'lover'. The whole
population wouldn't know who you mean. Why wouldn't the
whole population not know who you mean? Don't worry. Never
mind. Just say 'lover' like you know how I like to hear it.

> *(She can hardly stand now. He has to hurt her arm)*

BILLY: (barely) Lover.

INTRUDER: How come you're saying it like you don't mean it?

BILLY: Lover.

INTRUDER: Say it with pant-pant.

> *(He bounces himself violently against her. She cries out)*

BILLY: Lover!

INTRUDER: Again.

19

BILLY: *Lover!*

INTRUDER: Again, again!

BILLY: LOVER! LOVER!

(He steps back from her, abruptly, sadistically)

INTRUDER: Whoa. Don't be in a mad rush. Want, want.

(She sobs)

INTRUDER: I mean, why haven't you at least closed the
window? Hussy.
   (hissing into her ear)
Hussy.
   (and then)
But not right down. Why would you want him to go and miss
anything if he wakes up, would we? You and your secret lover.
   (forces her head to nod)
What did you say?
   (forces her head to shake no)
But you don't want to go on nodding and shaking your head, do
you? You want to put your hands behind your back.

BILLY: Please… I haven't been well.

INTRUDER: Oh, I know that.

(He forces her hands behind her back)

INTRUDER: (pressing against her again) You just hang onto
anything you want.

*(then viciously presses her hard up against the window,
pulls out a bit of cloth, with which he blindfolds her. Then
he turns her around to face him.)*

20

INTRUDER: I know. You'd just love to see me, run your eyes all over me. Talk to me with those eyes. Asking for it. But you like it better if you don't see me at first, don't you? Lick your lips and nod. You do that, pussy.

> *(She does so. He runs his hands over her, but lightly and discreetly)*

INTRUDER: I like you better with your clothes on. Do you know that? Covering yourself. Going around *taunting*. Day and night. But I'm not fussy. You're not fussy either, *underneath*, are you?
   (*command*)
You can tell me anything you want.

BILLY: Not fussy.

INTRUDER: You ought to be. Would I be here if you were some slag off the slag heap?

BILLY: Fussy. I'm... fussy.

INTRUDER: You're fussy with who you juice over, is it?

BILLY: I'm fussy with whom I juice over!

> *(He flings her angrily onto the bed)*

INTRUDER: Fucking liar!

BILLY: Please go away!

INTRUDER: Oh, it's games, is it? You're good at games. I think as soon as a man comes anywhere near you you start playing your games. That's what I think. Y'know what else I think? I think you're a nympho, but, me, I'm pure, so how would I know? Are you a nympho?
   (*she shakes her head*)
Oh, and there I was hoping I'd come across my first nympho.

21

BILLY: (quickly) I'm a nympho.

INTRUDER: (tone to hard) Then open your legs for my friend.

(She stiffens)

INTRUDER: My friend wants to meet you. I said open your legs
for my friend.
  (she does so)
Isn't that better? My friend's going to like that. You...

> *(His voice trails off unintelligibly once more; she tries to
> move away, but he hold he until he finishes jabbering,
> then:)*

INTRUDER: Well, get under the blankets then.
  (she does so; a sanctuary)
No, on your back. Pull up your nightie. All neat and nympho
tidy, like. You know just how far, don't you?

BILLY: What are you going to do?!

> *(He lashes out at her; she squeals)*

INTRUDER: I'll do you and him if you don't shut up.

> *(She lies rigid, fearfully waiting. But a smile only spreads
> across his face)*

INTRUDER: All I thought was you'd like to meet my friend.

BILLY: I don't...

INTRUDER: Go on, you know you do. It's all the more the
merrier with you, remember? Here, here. Come and meet my
friend...

> *(He takes her hand and guides it forcibly into his coat
> pocket, while he bends over her and kisses her on the neck.
> When she feels in his pocket, she stiffens, tries to pull her*

22

hand away, but he holds it in there)

INTRUDER: You like my friend. Hold on to my friend.

(He then guides her hand out. The blade of a gutting knife in her hands reflects sharply in the moonlight. It is only then that he straightens up from her neck.

He steps back. She is holding the knife up, trying to register what she is holding.

He hisses at her)

INTRUDER: *Yes. Harlot.*

(She stabs out in his direction but this is in more panic than targeting; she hasn't even taken the opportunity to remove her blindfold. He laughs at the ineffectuality of her gesture, then wrenches the knife out of her hand. Then prevents her from taking off the blindfold.

She moans as he sits astride her, the knife at her throat)

INTRUDER: (hissing) Don't tell me you believe what they write about me in the papers! Billy. See I know your pet name, don't I, Billy. You like the feel of my friend? Better than the real thing? And he isn't even your husband out there, is he?

BILLY: (thinly) I'll give you what you want.

INTRUDER: Of course you will.

BILLY: I will.

INTRUDER: (affecting disappointment) Aw,

BILLY: I… won't then.

INTRUDER: You sure?

BILLY: *Yes.*

INTRUDER: But I don't like it so much when I get what I want.

BILLY: *No, then.*

INTRUDER: Billy doesn't sound so sure. I think my friend and me are going to have to test Billy's sincerity.

BILLY: Don't hurt me.

INTRUDER: Not even a little bit?

BILLY. (now sobbing) No. *Yes.*

INTRUDER: I only want to hurt you a little bit, see. Like you let all the other men.

BILLY: No other men.

INTRUDER: You saying that only means I have to test your sincerity. I just don't like being lied to. My friend either.

BILLY: What do you want me to say?

INTRUDER: You don't have to say. You could whisper.

BILLY: Yes.

INTRUDER: Can't hear you.

BILLY: Yes.

INTRUDER: (angrily) Now you're *saying.*

BILLY: I don't know what you want me to say!

INTRUDER: All your other men.

BILLY: All right. Yes.

24

INTRUDER: Yes what?

BILLY: All my oth... *I can't.*

INTRUDER: You're not sincere at all, are you?

BILLY: You'll have to help me.

INTRUDER: And I thought you were being sincere with us.
With him lying out there and all.

BILLY: (attempt) Other men. Other men.

INTRUDER: You're not whispering.

(She can only just stop)

BILLY: No. I can't.

INTRUDER: Well, if you're not going to be sincere, I'll have
to... well, ask my friend.

*(He levers up the blankets on her legs with the blade of the
knife)*

INTRUDER: Let's see how my friend likes it with a harlot off the
streets...

*(and places, beneath the blankets, the blade against her
bare legs. She realizes what he is intending to do, cries out
and claws at the blindfold, then faints.*

Blackout)

4.

(BILLY regains consciousness. She does so with a start, tries to get the blindfold off.

The INTRUDER is now sitting at the end of the bed looking and smiling at her.

She freezes when he speaks)

INTRUDER: I think you'd rather not be able to see.

BILLY: (finally) What have you done?

INTRUDER: Why don't you feel for yourself?

(She probes herself carefully, discovers herself uninjured)

BILLY: Oh.

INTRUDER: No, nothing. Not yet. It wouldn't be polite if you're not around to enjoy it.

BILLY: What are you going to do with me?

INTRUDER: You? Don't tell me you've already forgotten about old Bill out there.

BILLY: (remembering, calls) Bill...?

(The INTRUDER goes to the window, looks out, turns back casually)

INTRUDER: Still breathing hard. Hard at what he's been hearing.
(laughs at his own joke, stops abruptly)
What my friend and I have decided to do, see, is help you out a bit.

BILLY: (false hope) Yes?

INTRUDER: Seeing as how you're not sincere and need... prodding... we're going to help you to tell us nice and sexily all about Arthur and Ben. There you are. Arthur and Ben. Right?

BILLY: Who?

INTRUDER: Arthur and Ben.

(She can only shake her head in confusion)

INTRUDER: Aw.

BILLY: (re blindfold) Can I take this off please?

INTRUDER: Jeez, be sincere when we've decided to be so helpful. Arthur and Ben. You remember Arthur and Ben. I do, and I've only been watching you for a few weeks. Watching Billy while she's been up on her goats, even.

BILLY: *How?*

INTRUDER: Wouldn't Billy and her Arthur and Ben like to know.

BILLY: *Filthy.*

(He grabs her ankles through the blankets, bangs them together painfully. His smile flashes)

INTRUDER: Arthur and Ben, Billy.

BILLY: I don't know what you're talking about. *Honestly.*

(He stands over her)

INTRUDER: (menacingly low now) We're giving you a chance to be sincere, aren't we?

BILLY: Listen. I… think you've got the wrong person. Please leave me alone.

INTRUDER: I've watched you wiggling everywhere. I've even lamped you when you've got old Bill out there panting for you to get back when Arthur and Ben have been crawling all over you. Disgusting. I was disgusted, wasn't I? Wasn't we? Say yes.

BILLY: Yes.

INTRUDER: Whisper yes.

BILLY: (doing so) Yes.

INTRUDER: (laughing) But don't go thinking my friend and I are trying to push you. We wouldn't want to spoil Billy's kicks, would we? We can wait.

BILLY: Wait?

INTRUDER: Wait for Billy to get sincere with us, what else?
   (*command*)
Roll over.

BILLY: No, please.

INTRUDER: Get over on your disgusting belly.

BILLY: What are you going to do?

INTRUDER: Aw, doesn't Billy want to play with her new friends?

> (*She now is getting up enough nerve to stare back at him with open defiance if not actual annoyance*)

INTRUDER: Get over!

> (*She does so, this time with exasperation*)

28

INTRUDER: Unspeakable. But we think Billy likes being unspeakable, doesn't she?

BILLY: (flatly) Billy likes being unspeakable.

INTRUDER: And I think Billy's soon going to call me Arthur.

BILLY: Arthur.

INTRUDER: Ben.

BILLY: Ben. Now do whatever you want and get out.

INTRUDER: Anything?

BILLY: Get out. You don't scare me anymore.

INTRUDER: But I didn't hear you say what I wanted.

(He lays the knife against her buttocks. She stifles a scream by biting onto the blankets. He sits back eventually to lean against the end of the bed again)

INTRUDER: Well, then, we've still got to wait until our Billy gets sincere.

(Long pause. Neither moves)

BILLY: For God's sake.

INTRUDER: We're still waiting.

BILLY: You bugger off.

INTRUDER: Why did you want to go and say that?

(Yet there is a tone now of unsureness in his voice. She senses he is losing impetus, even unto daring to turn her head slightly.

*He is glancing towards the window, almost shouts to
nobody)*

INTRUDER: Right up them. Both at the same time.

BILLY: Rubbish!

*(Having asserted herself to that degree, she tears off the
blindfold rag from around her neck.*

This coincides with a loud moan from BILL outside,

The INTRUDER stands up, on guard, knife at ready)

BILLY: (some hope at last) Bill!

*(The INTRUDER throws himself onto her and whispers
fiercely into her ear)*

INTRUDER: You wouldn't want old Bill to come in and get
over-excited, would you? See, he might accidentally try to move
out there and accidentally choke himself. Or I might have to go
out and stove his head in a bit. Just enough. Say, like an egg
shell?

BILLY: *What do you want*?

INTRUDER: Billy pussy, with all that *funnel.*

BILLY: What do you want me to do?

INTRUDER: Be sincere, why not?

BILLY: I'm thinking of Arthur and Ben, all right. Yes.

INTRUDER: And the thought of them is getting you all excited.

BILLY: Of course.

INTRUDER: And?

BILLY: And... Arthur and Ben mounting me. In and around.

INTRUDER: Behind whose back?

BILLY: Bill's!

INTRUDER: When, when?

BILLY: Whenever he's out. Whenever I can get it.

INTRUDER: Poor old Bill. Tired of old Bill.

BILLY: Yes.

INTRUDER: Say it properly and we're there.

BILLY: (whispering 'properly') Yes.

INTRUDER: There you go.

BILLY: Just... don't hurt.

INTRUDER: (shrugging) Well, one of you has to go.

BILLY: *No!*

INTRUDER: Of course one of you has to go. I've got a reputation to think of.

BILLY: No, no.

INTRUDER: But didn't you think it had to come to this? Mean, I'm only trying to be sincere from this end. I'll tell you about that old harpy a few months ago if you like, you being a harpy yourself, right? You wouldn't read about what I did to her. Well, maybe you did, ha ha. She was more than a bit like you, too, but at least she tried to be sincere. What really got up my goat was she wasn't putting enough effort into it. You know what I mean? It's really an insult when there's not enough *try*.

(*laughs*)
She tried after I tied her up like old Bill out there, but I really think, jeez, stiff, it was too late by then for my friend…

> (*He leans over and whispers in her ear. She dry retches, tries to move away from him but he holds her head until he has finished. Only then does he pull back*)

BILLY: Oh, God.

INTRUDER: I know you'd understand. On the other hand, what's old Bill out there? He's going to choke or suffocate. And anyway, weren't you going to ditch him over for Arthur and Ben? Weren't we?
(*to her shake of the head:*)
Sure you were. So just say 'him' and fair enough with me, 'kay?
(*suddenly hard*)
Chose!

> (*She struggles but he is too strong for her. Finally, she has to say something but it comes out unintelligibly:*)

INTRUDER: Can't hear you.

BILLY: (sobbing) Him.

> (*He becomes sexually agitated, begins to fondle her and doesn't notice the window being opened carefully*)

INTRUDER: Not loud enough. Pump it out. *Pump* it. So I can hear it through your panting….

BILLY: Him…

INTRUDER: *Pump it up and down!*

> (*BILL gets through the window and throws himself on the man with the advantage of coming from behind.*
>
> *They reel and fight madly over the knife. Its blade flashes*

32

in the moonlight.

Blackout)

5.

(Lighting up from the reading lamp.

The INTRUDER is picking himself gingerly up from the floor. Slowly, the lighting reveals him to be TIM.

BILL stands over him with the knife at the ready, obviously fighting an impulse to plunge it into the younger man.

BILLY cries out to him not to. But then, BILL swings around to her. For a moment, the knife points at her. Then BILL bellows and throws it far out of the window.

A long and tension'd pause. BILL stares at her; in turn she searches his eyes for a reason, trying to understand.

In the meantime, TIM rises painfully.)

TIM: What'd you do that for?

BILL: You went too far.

TIM: I was doing my best. It wasn't easy.

BILLY: (confused) 'Trying'?

BILL: (rounds on her) You shut it.

TIM: (still at BILL) What's gotten into you?

BILL: (back at him) You take off.

33

TIM: What'd you expect me to do?

BILL: What you said you'd do. Get going.

TIM: I didn't see you trying to stop it.

BILLY: What's going on?

BILL: You're what's fucking going on!

(She looks from one man to the other, registers situation)

BILLY: I don't believe it.

TIM: (laughs) She thinks I did pretty well.

BILLY: *Why?*

TIM: (smirk) Why, she asks.

BILL: I told you to take off.

TIM: I only got a bit mad when she started to enjoy it, Bill. You heard.

BILL: I heard you too. I heard both of you.

TIM: She couldn't unload you quick enough.

BILLY: You're both… *sick.*

(and decides to flail out at BILL. As soon as she does so, however, he too loses his control, flails back at her. He almost lifts her off the floor, shaking her like a pup, and shouting obscenities. Finally, he flings her back onto the bed, where she lies still, just as fearful as before.

TIM snorts derision behind BILL's back. BILL swings around to him and speak with extra menace:)

BILL: You piss off and piss off real quick, sonny jim.

TIM: I don't think you heard all of it.

BILL: You've got two seconds flat.

> *(Pause as they stare at each other. Then TIM reluctantly turns and leaves. We hear the front door being slammed behind him.*
>
> *A long silence, before:)*

BILLY: (sotto voce) After what I've been through… you could play that dirty trick on me?

BILL: Balls.

BILLY: That was sick. I was sick.

BILL: Balls. Balls is all you've been through.

> *(Pause while they quieten somewhat. They go into their own private thoughts.*
>
> *This moment extends beyond just a long silence but becomes a reluctance on each's part to return to the world of their union)*

BILL: We had an agreement.

BILLY: And I kept to it.

BILL: That old hammock out there's gone all black and rotten suddenly.

BILLY: (hotly) What's that got to do with anything?

BILL: (bitterly) You had to have men.

BILLY: We've been through all this.

35

BILL: You and your out in the open. It hasn't worked out for me.

BILLY: (now feeling she can take the ascendency) You're not kidding there. I told you, there's still you and me.

BILL: *Jesus, I heard you.*

BILLY: *He hurt me.*

    (A pause towards calm)

BILLY: (bland statement) He hurt me.

BILL: I'll talk to him later.

BILLY: Did you know what his mind is really like?

BILL: What do you care? I'll talk to him later, I said.

    (But she continues to look accusingly at him. He starts to get angry again)

BILL: I told you your sordid stuff was your sordid stuff.

BILLY: No, you didn't!

BILL: Christ, if I thought you were laughing at me behind my back with other guys…

BILLY: Never.

BILL: Never, ratshit. This Arthur and Ben. Where'd they come from?

BILLY: I don't know any Arthur or Ben. I told him!

BILL: Who's Arthur and Ben?

BILLY: Nobody's listening to me!

(throwing it back on him)
You went too far.

BILL: You went too far! I went along with it providing no names ever.
 (and)
You want to know how I could do that to you? I think I lost my respect for you a long time ago. Like you, me, apparently.

BILLY: No, I never have. Not until now.

BILL: (murderously) You were going to let me choke to death out there just to save your own neck.

BILLY: (outcry) He was going to hurt me!
 (quickly follows up with:)
I haven't only disgusted you. I've disgusted me too.
 (and)
What I wanted to say to you down here this weekend... do you think you could forget all the nonsense I was talking about? Do you think we could maybe start over again?

(He at least turns his eyes away from hers)

BILL: It's too late for me to promise anything anymore.

(She nods and crawls back under the blankets.

He follows, switches off the reading lamp to flood the room with moonlight once more.

They lie side by side, their eyes open)

BILL: (softly but firmly) I had to find out about those two.

BILLY: You could've asked me. You bet.

BILL: I did ask you.

BILLY: I'd remember if you did.

37

BILL: Yeah, and that's the answer I thought I'd get.

(There follows a long pause)

BILL: What's it like to be toyed with like that? You don't have to answer.

BILLY: Horrible.

BILL: All of it?

BILLY: There's some sort of tingle. I suppose. I don't know. It's been a long time.

BILL: (matter-of-factly) Beneath it all, you're a bit of a slut, you know that?

BILLY: Maybe.

BILL: (quiet command) Open your legs like he told you to.

BILLY: (surprise) You?

BILL: Open your legs like he told you to.

(She looks at him unerringly, but he still stares ahead. She does what he has asked)

BILLY: Oh, yes, please.

(They make love.

They do not see the figure that appears outside the window to watch them doing so.

Blackout)

(End Act 1)

Act 2
6.

(Ten minutes later.

They lie apart. Both are still awake, indicating their love-making has been less than satisfactory)

BILL: *Hopeless.*

BILLY: Let's not go into all that again, love.

BILL: Sure?

BILLY: I'm never unhappy.
  (follows pause)
You know, I feel more potentially self-defined than I have in weeks. Would you read about that? No, I'm not *saying* it happily. I hate it. It's detestable feeling yourself on tap again, that's all. Maybe toppling over is just natural for me and I haven't accepted it. Do you think I ever will?

  (BILL sits up, having heard something)

BILL: Quiet a moment.

  (He gets up to look out of the window. There is something, some movement about somewhere...a rhythmic tapping against the side of the bungalow and a growing discernable breathing.

  When a shadow moves past the window, they both start)

BILLY: Oh, no.

BILL: You saw it?

BILLY: (accusing him) Enough, Bill, please.

BILL: Forget that. You see something?

BILLY: I think. I'm not sure anymore.

> *(She goes to switch on lamp again)*

BILL: Don't do that.
  (then)
I'm still hearing something. You phone emergencies.

BILLY: Where's the phone?

BILL: I don't know!

BILLY: (fearfully, can't go) I think I left it in the kitchen or something.

BILL: Why?!

BILLY: How do I know?

BILL: You stay here.

> *(He takes dressing table torch, ventures outside.*
>
> *She waits fearfully, spooked by every little sound he makes out there.*
>
> *He returns after what for her is an eternity. He is holding the mobile phone like it is a useless thing)*

BILL: What'd you do with the battery?

BILLY: Nothing!

BILL: That stupid idiot Tim!

> *(He sits on the bed with her, both listening hard.*

Someone seems to move down the passageway. BILL jumps up and hurries out in a fit of bravery.

This leaves BILLY alone again. This time is worse; the worst possibilities obviously loom in her mind, become near panic. Finally, she manages to croak out...)

BILLY: Bill...?

(A figure frames itself in the doorway. She cries out before she realizes it is only BILL)

BILL: It's me.

BILLY: What was it?

BILL: Dunno. Forget it. I couldn't...

(He gets no further as, simultaneous to her warning cry, another figure wearing overcoat and hat lunges from behind BILL and hits him brutally on the back of the head with the butt of a shotgun.

BILL is felled, doesn't move.

Before she can scream, the INTRUDER shoves the barrel of the weapon against BILL's head meaningfully)

BILLY: Tim...?

(But the man neither answers nor shift his gaze from her)

BILLY: Who are you?

(The INTRUDER laughs at her, nods. His tone of it is psychotic, sadistic. A wolfish grin spreads across his face when he sees how helpless she is. He straightens from BILL, moves carefully, stalkingly, towards her.

She tries to back away but is hampered by being on the bed.
He stops a few feet away. She can feel his menace, his eyes
running up and down her. She shudders)

BILLY: (barely able to) Oh, don't...

(The man reaches out towards her night dress. Her instinct
is that he is going to tear it off. She tries to protect herself,
but instead he drops the back of his hand lightly onto her
thigh. Then withdraws his hand and smells it.

She tries to control her breath, but he grabs her by the arm,
forces her back on the bed, then points to her to lie there.

When she has quietened somewhat he roughly rolls her over
onto her stomach. She is suffering too much shock to resist
very much. He puts down the shotgun and begins to tie her
wrists but his sexual excitement is such that he is fumbling
the task. His face is sinking closer and closer to her neck.

It gives her time to gather herself a little. She suddenly
jerks her head backwards to smash into the side of his. He
reels back in reaction. She tries to roll over to escape, but
he grabs her with one hand. She can wrench herself away
from this, grabs for the gun and turns to face him with it)

BILLY: You... horrible...

(But the moment she might have used the weapon has
passed and they both know it. He grins slowly and
confidently, re-imposing his advantage over her. He
advances slowly. Her aim wavers. He is able to simply
take the weapon away from her, puts it down gloatingly and
takes a 'loaded' step towards her.

BILLY throws herself under the bed, regains the gun.

He laughs, then goes after her. At first he is too confident
and crawls towards her on all fours, but she strikes him a
glancing blow to the face with the weapon. Only then is he

42

enraged. He tries to grab her but she slides away to the other side of the bed, tries from a different angle. She easily avoids him. It is getting ridiculous, were it not for the face she is getting closer and closer at hitting him very hard with the shotgun each time he tries.

He changes his attack by grabbing hold of her ankle, but the rifle is long enough for her to nearly strikes his wrist. He tries around the bed, but even the footboard is too low for him to reach her safely.

What he thought was going to be easy has now become ridiculously difficult. His frustration begins translating itself into an agitated uncertainty, then into outright rage.

He tries to 'dummy' her out of position by changing sides and directions but still cannot get hold of any part of her before she strikes out and manages to wriggle away from his reach.

At one lunge he is able to grab the gun's muzzle but in the ensuing tug-of-war she easily wins even this by levering her feet. When she rips the gun from him, his hand is badly torn. He cries out in pain.

The man is now in a blind rage. He bellows and attacks the bed itself, tearing off the mattress and exposing her beneath the springs. It still doesn't help him much; in fact it is making it even harder to get any purchase on her or the gun. In rage, he starts bouncing the bed up and down, side to side, but she is able to hang on to it by the springs to prevent him from toppling it off her.

He has to step back to regain his breath. It is a vital pause for her, allowing her to recover some vital small amount too.

After the hiatus, he backs off and goes back to the prone figure of BILL, takes him by the throat and shakes him like a rabbit. Then stops and looks meaningfully at her, to come

43

out.

But she is too collected now and stubbornly refuses to come out from under the protection of the bed. In return, she aims the gun at him from beneath there – and this time it is with real and obvious intent. Her aim is perfectly steady.

It is an impasse. The INTRUDER finally realizes her determination despite anything he might do to BILL. In the hope of surprise he throws himself along the floor at her, makes another grab for the gun. Her instinctive reaction is effective; she has jerked the weapon upwards and it strike him painfully in the chest.

He writhes in pain. As he does so, she gets out from under the bed on the other side from him and tries to make a break for it but he is lucky to be able to grab hold of her with one hand.

She tears herself out of his grip and, realizing she probably can't get past him, retreats back to under the bed.

They both lie back spent, trying to recover. But both are thinking hard.

Blackout)

7.

(Same positions.

The INTRUDER shrugs his shoulders and laughs. This time it projects pleasantness. He leans over to switch on the lamp, laughs again when that doesn't work)

TIM: (revealing himself and urbanely) Forgot I pulled the main switch.

BILLY: Tim?

TIM: One and only, Billy.

> *(He removes and impediment to recognizing him, smiles at her innocently)*

BILLY: You little bastard!

TIM: Hey, don't go getting the wrong idea, Billy.

BILLY: (unbelievably) What?

TIM: Hey, come on. Come out from there and look.

> *(She refuses to move. Now he shows genuine embarrassment)*

TIM: Billy. *Listen.* What Bill said to do. Don't go crazy thinking something else.
(in BILL's direction)
Tell her, Bill.

> *(But BILL doesn't move)*

BILLY: What've you done to him?

TIM: *Nothing.*
(back at BILL)
Hey, quit fooling around. Bill! You straighten this lady out.

> *(He goes to move over to BILL but she cuts his movement short by threatening with the gun even from the cover of the bed)*

BILLY: You stay put.

TIM: *Bill.*

(He gets no reply. He swings back to her appealing)

TIM: I don't know what's going on between you two. For sure.
Hey, you've got to believe me, Billy. Why would I do that? You
wanna be careful with that thing.
　(but her aim doesn't waver)
Okay, Billy, I'll take off like you said. You sort it out with your
husband.

BILLY: (now cold and calculated) Like you said, he isn't my
husband,

TIM: I don't know what you're playing at. I'm getting out.

BILLY: Look at him!

TIM: He's kidding! I didn't really hit him, for chrissakes. Think,
Billy.
　(not getting anywhere)
It's your nerves. He said that it'd be your nerves.

BILLY: (coldly) Did he? Did you say that, Bill?

　　　*(Still BILL doesn't move. But at least it's encouragement
　　　for TIM)*

TIM: That's right. You ask him. Just let me go, okay?

BILLY: Oh, I don't think so.

TIM: Jesus, Bill. That's far enough, man.
　(back to her)
Listen, Billy, come out.

　　　(She still refuses to. He doesn't know what to do now)

TIM: Hell.
　(then)

46

It was a put-up job like last time, Billy. You get onto him what
for. Okay, I'm sorry. But I don't know what he's playing at,
unless he somehow hit his head or something. Hey, it's between
you two, alright?
(*no answer*)
I'm out of here, okay? You can't stop me. No shooting,
chrissakes.

BILLY: (coldly) All you're going to do is get out there and turn
the lights back on, and then you're coming back here.

TIM: Sure. All right.

(He hurries out of the bedroom.

*When she is sure he is gone, she crawls out from under the
bed. It is noticeable she keeps the gun pointed at BILL,
though)*

BILLY: Now you can get up too.

*(Yet still BILL doesn't move. She inches forward, reaches
out with the shotgun and prods him. He doesn't flinch at
all.*

*She inches forward and pulls him roughly over onto his
back.*

His face is covered with blood.

*She cries out, barely has time to realise the implications,
before TIM launches himself from the passageway and onto
her. She back pedals frantically towards the bed again and
manages to get half under it. But now he has her by both
legs and is succeeding in pulling her back.*

*But when he releases one foot to reach for, and succeed in
getting the gun, she is able to kick him off and to regain the
sanctity of the bed.*

47

Now he is in an absolute rage. He throws himself on all fours, points the weapon at her)

TIM: Come out or else.

(Yet he is obviously too murderous now for that to be any possibility. BILLY can only shake her head. In fury, he climbs on top of the bed, aims down at her face. This new 'visibility' calms both of them down slightly. It has something to do with accessibility. Instead he leers down at her)

TIM: Should have thought of the bird's-eye view before, shouldn't I? Say yes, Billy.

BILLY: You want me to whisper it, you *sick*?

TIM: Billy oughtn't to speak to me like that. Not a family playmate.

BILLY: You dirty little maniac.

TIM: Oh, Billy, Billy.

BILLY: You filthy little nothing.

(At this he stiffens)

BILLY: Go rot in hell.

(He flies into another rage, and tries to get at her again. Endeavouring to heave the bed off her has the same result as before. All he can do is lift one side and kick at her but this is not effective in making her let go the springs from underneath. He can, too, hit away at her fingers, but he has to let the bed 'go' to do so, which allows her to do so too.

Yet again he has to stop in futility. He steps back to recover his senses.

48

Then smiles and sits on the end of the bed. In this position he is virtually sitting on top of her. He can now laugh at her.

This infuriates her now. She does her best to rock the bed to throw him 'off' her, but this is as ineffective as his attempts.

He rides her furious rocking like a buck jumper, hamming it up.

She has to stop, exhausted)

TIM: Hey, don't stop. Give us a real good buck, Billy. You buck. That's what you know how to do, right? I ought to know. Haven't we been watching her bucking, bucking for years, anytime, night and day, up here or back in town? Billy bucking up and down. So it's our turn, I reckon. Buck. Go on, *buck.*

(She meets his stare with hatred in her eyes. It brings home to him, however belatedly, the gap between the reality of her and the fantasy he has of her. He can only almost whine:)

TIM: It's my turn.

BILLY: You have to be joking.

TIM: I've waited long enough!

BILLY: That's revolting.
  (*calls*)
Bill?

TIM: (waves that off) I said it's my turn.

(and levels the gun to her head with added meaning this time)

BILLY: No, don't.

49

TIM: Who's turn is it to buck?

BILLY: Yours.

TIM: Whose?

BILLY: Tim's.

TIM: (getting aroused by it) That's better. I like that better.
 (then)
But Billy wouldn't want to have me like that, would she?
 (she doesn't understand)
In that position.

        (She opens her legs)

TIM: Exactly. Billy knows exactly what a man wants, doesn't
she? Legs open and feeling better already, isn't she? Billy should
say pretty please.

BILLY: Please.

TIM: She should be saying it like I am up here and I'd puke all
over the joint to think of having it off with an old slag like her.
And the old slag aching for it from me. Say it again. Like you're
old and disgusting and all you can do is beg for it.

BILLY: All I can do is beg for it.

TIM: Who're you talking to?

BILLY: Tim.
 (to his orchestration)
All I can do is beg for it, Tim.

        (Long pause while he stares blandly down at her. His
        sadistic smile fades. She notices how this is so and closes
        her legs quickly)

50

TIM: I think I'm going to shoot you now, Billy. I really think I am.

BILLY: (near fainting) No...

TIM: Oh, yes.

(She can only watch his finger tighten on the trigger.

He shoots, but there is only the click of the hammer.

She sobs.

Blackout)

8.

(Moonlight, immediately after.

BILLY is sobbing and taking great gulps of air. She is so obviously at the end of her tether that he could easily pull her out from under the bed. But he doesn't do so. He remains sitting on the end of the bed, literally sitting on top of her.

A cloud passes over the moon, casting the whole room in barely discernible gloom. Just before it does so, we see TIM opening his coat and his hands begin to caress himself)

TIM: Belly. Slide. Belly. Slide. Belly... yes, I was there, yes, I was there, *yes*...

(Blackout)

9.

(Lighting from reading lamp back on.

She is now laughing openly up at him. He is slumped over and momentarily in quietus)

BILLY: Lover. Big deal rapist. You ought to see how feeble you look from down here. Yes, little boy. Little boy was there. Big deal.

TIM: Don't.

BILLY: (mimic) Don't.
 (*then*)
I never did things like that, little boy. It's all in your head, you know that?

TIM: I don't want you to talk like that.

BILLY: He doesn't want me to talk like that.

TIM: I've said don't talk to me like that.

BILLY: Finish it then. You can't, can you?

TIM: I won't tell you again.

BILLY: Poor little bugger knows it too. Now, get off my bed, sicko!

(He flies into another rage, screeching as he jumps up and down on the springs over her and trying to stomp her face beneath his feet.

She cries out with alarm at first but soon realizes that he is impotent in this too. She merely lies still and begins to snigger up at him.

He stops.

A look of absolute finality passes across his face. When he speaks, his voice takes on the psychotic tone it had before)

TIM: Now why would Billy want to talk to us like that?

(He brings out the knife from his pocket again)

BILLY: You're joking.

TIM: Old slags have no right to go around the world corrupting, corrupting. Smelling and not washing off. That's what we think, isn't it? Oh, yes, it is.

(He suddenly drops onto the springs and plunges the knife down through them at her. He stabs manically, time and time again.

BILLY screams, tries to writhe away but is being stabbed, if only superficially, when she tries to push the bed back against him. Finally, she manages to heave upwards enough to catch him off balance. The bed spills over and traps him half beneath him. It allows her to escape out through the window.

He flings the bed off. By now she has gone. He takes stock of the situation. For a moment it looks like he is contemplating attacking BILL, but then leaps out of the window after her.

Blackout)

(End Act 2)

Act 3
10.

(Half an hour later.

All the lights are on. Everything has been restored to order… the bed remade with only the disarrangement of it indicating it has been slept in.

BILL is sitting with his head between his legs, obviously just coming around from being knocked out.

TIM is kneeling beside him, wiping his face with a damp cloth. He has discarded the overcoat and hat again and is now dressed in pyjama bottom and dressing gown. He is affecting shock over what has happened. It is a good cover for his agitation.

There is no sign of BILLY)

TIM: (solicitous) Can't you remember anything?

(BILL can only shake his head painfully)

TIM; I just think you should let me ring for the police or something, Bill. I would've. But I thought I'd wait until you came to. Just as well, if you're sure you don't want them.

BILL: Where's Billy?

TIM: Around. Don't worry about her.

(BILL waves his hand to go and get her.

TIM goes out of the room to do so.

When he has gone, BILL gets to his feet without too much trouble. He notices blood on the floor rug and then under

54

the bed.

TIM returns)

TIM: She must've gone out for a bit. Don't ask me why.
  (*then*)
The phone's dead.

BILL: No batteries. He must have taken them.

TIM: I'll go and get my phone.

BILL: Wait.

TIM: You said 'he'. You mean Billy didn't take them?

BILL: Just tell me where she is.

TIM: I don't know. All I know is she's all right.

BILL: You must have scared him off.

TIM: Well, when I came running, *I* sure scared her off, I think.

BILL: How long have I been out?

TIM: Dunno. All we heard over there was a scream.

BILL: You didn't see anything? You didn't see Billy?

TIM: I saw the back of her. Then the moon went. Then I heard
you. What's going on?

BILL: Just tell me where she went.

TIM: Take it easy, Bill.

BILL: *Jesus.*

TIM: You want to tell me?

BILL: That maniac must have been around here all the time. Watching. Got me from behind.
  (*to the other's look of amazement*)
That maniac we used as a cover. The *real* one.

TIM: Can't be.

BILL: You must have scared him off.
  (*then*)
You only saw Billy, nobody else?

TIM: Who knows, out there? Maybe, when I think of it.

BILL: Think.

TIM: *Maybe*.

BILL: BILLY?

TIM: She's gone, Bill. Let her go.

BILL: Gone? What's gone?

TIM: (smirk) She must have really flipped after our little effort, right?

BILL: What the hell are you talking about?

TIM: Buggering up the phone. Screaming around the place. Busting your head. Sorry about that.

BILL: I just told you it was him.

TIM: Hey, come on.

BILL: Now, you just start from the word go. What happened to your face? Where's Billy? What do you mean 'let her go'?

TIM: You serious? Look, I know nothing from nothing. I was home getting into bed when I heard this scream from over here. My mum too. I didn't take any notice, knowing Billy. But then I hear this second one, so I get Dad's gun. By the time I got here you were out on the floor and the place empty. I realized it must have been Billy when I thought I saw someone running off.
(*cunningly*)
You say the real intruder. What's the odds, Bill. I mean... you know... her running off like that, not coming over to my place for help. Well, see, I thought she must have done this to you....? Mean, the way she came at me out of the dark, the lights turned off here.

BILL: You said you only saw her running away.

TIM: No, I didn't. She came at me as soon as I fronted. Really. She must have been out of her mind, the way she was screaming, punching, tearing Dad's gun out of my hands. Look at the gash.

BILL: (warningly) You'd better tell me where she is.

TIM: I told you. She took off down the road. She'll be down at the other blocks by now. She'll be okay.

(*Pause*)

BILL: (remorse) I've let something loose.

TIM: She must have been scared out of her wits, I'll give you that. I just thought she'd heard what was going on from you and was mad at me for doing what you wanted.

BILL: No.

TIM: You mean that pervert bugger was watching all the time?

BILL: I... don't know.

TIM: It stands to reason when you think about it. Incredible.

57

BILL: What do you mean?

TIM: Why she came out tearing at me. She must have been hiding in the bushes, thought I was him, and came at me from behind. Why else? Don't you go thinking you didn't see him.
   (*then*)
Oh God, we're not thinking. She'll already be on the phone. She'll be bringing the police, Bill!

BILL: (now alarmed for self too) You sure you saw here going off down the road?

TIM: Where else?
   (*but thinks about it*)
They're going to think that madman is me!
   (*then*)
I'll go out and look around!

   (*But BILL holds him back*)

BILL: Hold it. Let's think.

   (*TIM makes a show of doing so*)

BILL: It's like you first came the crap on to me. You heard a scream and found me lying here. I know nothing. You know nothing. Let's not go over-embellishing.

TIM: Then why did she fly at me like that?

BILL: Didn't I just say you know nothing? Anyway, like you said, you think she must have mistaken you for the real thing.

TIM: The real thing? 'Embellishing'?

BILL: Don't get smart.

TIM: You said I wouldn't get involved in anything.

BILL: Chrissakes, listen! You know nothing.

58

(thinks further)
But that's the thing. You've got to be sure you saw him running after her. And you... came to get me instead of going after him, her.

TIM: Well, I am. I'm pretty sure, as I say, now I think about it.

BILL: Yeah, well, you stick to that.

TIM: No, I mean for real.
   (low cunning)
And that's alright for me, but what about you?

BILL: What're you going on about?

TIM: No, say, we're both right in fact. You said it must have been him. I'm saying I'm now pretty sure I saw someone chasing after her, could only have been him... right? So, where does that leave you. Mean, that means, he's here and he's watching us all the time. What we did.

BILL: Go on.

TIM: That means he must have moved in on her after I left. He gets in... she's all batty... he's watching where you are and he gets you first... before, you know, Billy.

BILL: (a real possibility) *Shit, are you sure you saw her running off?*

TIM: You mean the other thing?

BILL: Did you look around?

TIM: How?

BILL: You saw him running off. You get to me.

TIM: I tidied the place up a bit, I shouldn't have.

BILL: I don't mean fucking that! Did you look around for her?!

TIM: *Bill, she was off her nut*!

BILL: (stopping) What's that got to do with it?

TIM: (outcry) How do I know?

> *(BILL goes to the window, looks out, calls for BILLY, but of course gets no response. He turns back:)*

BILL: We're going to have to tell them everything.

TIM: She's going to nail me! You promised!

BILL: I didn't know that sick shit was going to be around.
Watching, *watching*. Jesus!
  (*changes mind again*)
We stick to we-know-nothing.

TIM: What about her?

BILL: If she was… what'd you say…?

TIM: Batty?

BILL: Batty. Then they'll see her imagination would have come into it.

TIM: (relief) Unreliable.

BILL: Yeah, unreliable.

TIM: Silly bitch.

BILL: Yeah, but I can say that, sonny. You can't. You don't even think it.

TIM: I was just thinking all the things she confessed to.

BILL: (still hard) You don't even think about that either. It was a game.

TIM: Okay.

(BILL goes and sits on bed, head in hands. He is, after all, sick and sorry.

TIM comes over and sits next to him. He puts his hand on BILL's shoulder in a telltale familiar way.

BILL shrugs his touch off)

BILL: Forget that too. You just get your story right or you could find yourself on another bed, boy. It's called a bunk behind bars.

(TIM gets up very deliberately and goes over to pick up his overcoat, puts hand in pocket and keeps it there; turns back coldly to BILL)

TIM: What do you mean by that?

BILL: I mean that if that joker out there needed a few extra lessons on how to about about it, you gave him plenty to think about.
    (*and*)
You had yourself a few extra kicks, didn't you? You've got all the makings, matey. Come to think of it, you sure it happened like you say?

(He has a spasm of concussion pain, put his head back into his hands. TIM moves almost imperceptibly to be around behind him)

BILL: (managing without looking up) And why the gun? Where did all that presence of mind come from? I'd like to know another thing, too.

TIM: (voice changed to menacing) Ask away.

61

BILL: Why haven't you gone back and phoned for help from your place?

TIM: No batteries?

BILL: You being smart-arsed now?

TIM: I told you I was waiting for you to decide what our story's going to be.

BILL: You let her panic, escape. I decided a long time ago.

TIM: (loaded meaning) We wouldn't want to go out there if he's still around, would we?

BILL: (showing so by his side) I've got the shotgun.

TIM: Not loaded, is it?

BILL: He doesn't know that.

TIM: Oh, I think he might.

> *(BILL has another dizzy spell, holds his head, sways. TIM smoothly takes the gun away from his side, holds it above BILL ready to strike)*

TIM: Do we still deny everything?

BILL: Still thinking about it…

> *(This has signed his death warrant. TIM raises the shotgun and is about to bring it down when:*
>
> *A piercing scream from well outside.*
>
> *BILL stands upright. TIM drops the gun.*
>
> *Blackout)*

(Through the darkness, there is a strangled cry for BILL. It is a woman's voice.)

11.

(Instantaneous lighting up. A moment to react, then BILL grabs the gun and runs out.

On hearing it, TIM stops still, waits, thinking hard.

We hear BILL rushing out of doors, hear him calling for BILLY.

Then relative silence.

TIM begins to become uneasy. This time the silence around begins to work on him. He begins to hear noises. He goes to the window, calls out for some reply, but it doesn't come.

When another cloud passes over the moon, the resulting and dense eeriness takes hold of him. He pulls his head in quickly, goes over to close the bedroom door.

He goes back for the gun, remembers that BILL has taken it.

The lights go out suddenly. He is alone in the darkness.

Blackout)

12.

(The cloud passes from the moon. Moonlight floods the room again. But it doesn't help TIM's feeling very much alone.

He swings around through instinct. The INTRUDER is there. It is shocking, stultifying to TIM.

They stand looking at each other... the one grinning wolfishly, the other in shock.

The INTRUDER's hand slowly goes to the pocket of the coat he has somehow got in the darkness and put on; the movement is deliberate, malevolent. He draws out the knife sensuously, its blade again reflecting in the moonlight.

Now in the grip of fear himself, TIM can only take a few steps backwards.

The INTRUDER sniggers at him; it is personal and contemptuous. When he speaks the voice is pathological, unreal)

INTRUDER: I saw you.

(then sniggers again. That is all that is said between them but the atmosphere is heavy with TIM's shock and with the INTRUDER's threat.

The INTRUDER moves forward slowly, moving the knife in slow circles. He has almost crossed the room before TIM can get moving and, in blind panic, hurls himself into a corner of the room, his panic and fear breaking out openly. The INTRUDER smiles knowingly and closes in.

It is all TIM can do to watch the knife come into his face, then to slowly run down his body until it stops against his groin.

He blindly tries to break past but the INTRUDER easily pitches him to the floor.

TIM's state is such that it does not occur to him that the situation literally echoes the scene between him and BILLY. The INTRUDER is standing over him now and goading him with the point of the knife.

Frantically, TIM makes for the cover of the bed. The INTRUDER does little to try to stop him; he only shoves the blankets and mattress off one corner of the bed to expose a good part of TIM... as he had done to BILLY... under the springs.

The INTRUDER slowly raises the knife. TIM whimpers with terror and is helpless when the knife is plunged down at him repeatedly... again, as he had done to BILLY.

At that moment the thin slither of moonlight passes and the room is plunged into darkness again)

13.

(After the briefest blackout, the moonlight increases steadily to allow almost full vision.

There is no INTRUDER.

Very carefully, TIM crawls out from under the bed. No-one. He jumps to his feet, is about to run for the door when a shadow falls across him from the doorway. He freezes.

Then BILL moves into the room)

BILL: What're you doing?

TIM: (hatred) You. It was you.

BILL: (ignores that) I could have sworn I kept hearing her.

(TIM looks but can't find any weapon to hit back with)

TIM: It was you.

BILL: Hey, pull yourself together. What's wrong with you?

TIM: You!

(But he double takes when he notices that the mattress and blankets are back in place. He looks sharply at BILL, then shuts his mouth and turns away)

BILL: Don't you start now. Shit, it's bad enough.

TIM: (surly but wavering) I know it was you. It couldn't have been...

(He won't or can't say it. BILL grabs him, turns him around to face him)

BILL: Hey, you're not kidding, are you? You tell me what happened!

TIM: *I don't know.*

BILL: Snap out of it!

TIM: *What were you trying to do to me?*

BILL: Billy?

TIM: No! Where were you?

BILL: Someone was in here?

TIM: Yes!

BILL: You sure it wasn't Billy?

TIM: *Yes.*

BILL: Then I wasn't hearing things. He must have Billy out there somewhere. What's he want?

(He goes to go out again)

BILL: Keep the lights on, shitsake.

TIM: Why'd you switch them off?

BILL: (stopping) Wasn't me.
  (*then*)
Christ! Come on!

(He hurries out, but TIM doesn't, can't, follow. He listens to BILL fumbling around in the other rooms)

BILL: The fuses have been pulled!

(Then there comes BILLY's sobbing from outside somewhere.

Then silence.

TIM is left alone once more. He has become almost frozen with fearful anticipation. Again, he hears sounds around... scratching, movements, breathing. He backs into the corner again, hunches. The sounds are getting closer, becoming more personal. Little boy, I saw you, little boy... repeated over and over, becoming more distinct, becoming more hissed and laced with unintelligible obscenities.

The whispering ends with a forceful thumping on the bungalow's wall from outside but right above his head. It makes him whimper before he can control himself.

Then silence.

But he dares not move. He is crouched now, small and vulnerable.

A shout from BILL, off. Then another, more urgent. TIM still can't move)

BILL: (off) Tim! I've got her over here!

(TIM is visibly relieved. He jumps up, goes to the window, looks out.

In the now clear moonlight he sees BILL obviously struggling to life BILLY.

TIM hurries out to help.

Blackout)

14

(They carry BILLY into the bedroom.

By her appearance it seems obvious that she has suffered trauma and is in a bad way... far worse than when she escaped from TIM. Her nightdress is torn and she is barely conscious.

When she does speak, it is barely audible and reflects numbing distress.

She is clinging to BILL, is shunning TIM. But then neither is she showing any fear of the younger man.

They put her gently onto the bed, where she lies motionless.

They look down at her, not knowing what to do – BILL with his jaw set; TIM with utter confusion)

TIM: (hiss) I didn't do that.

BILL: You've got to go for help.

TIM: (gets implications) No.

BILL: Chrissakes, run fast. Take the gun. Anything. But go.

TIM; The gun's not loaded.

BILL: (stopping) How do you know?

TIM: I just do.

BILL: What does it matter? *Go.*

TIM: Where is it?

(They both stop, look around)

BILL: Did you take it outside?

TIM: Did you? I was carrying her!

BILL: What I'm saying. Did you leave it out there?

TIM: *He must have it.*

(A shocked pause)

BILL: We ought to wait here... until she comes round, or it gets light.

BILLY: (suddenly) Arthur?!

(and tries to struggle upwards. BILL holds her down until

she quietens, and she is looking at him with wide-open quizzical eyes.

Then she smiles sweetly and vacuously at him – a little girl)

BILLY: Arthur.

BILL: It's Bill, love.

BILLY: Hello, Arthur. I know what you want.

(She swings her eyes onto TIM. He expects accusation but instead she smiles just as sweetly and vacuously)

BILLY: My Ben.

(She holds his hand. As surreptitiously as he can, he makes her let go)

BILLY: My Arthur and Benny boy. Oh, and the damp is so chilly on the ground. No, on my back, you sillies. Frost spikes, yours, ha ha. We must find a place warm and humming. Soft as a mattress. Is a tongue.

(She lies back, closes her eyes)

BILL: I don't want to know about this.

TIM: What're we going to do?

BILL: (bitterly) Let her bloody Arthur and Ben help her.

TIM: (seeing escape possibility) That's what I say.
   (then)
We going to leave her?
   (BILL shrugs; TIM goes Iago like)
We could just say that nothing you said. We don't know how she got back here. She wasn't here when we left.

(BILL pushes him away)

70

TIM: Don't do that. *She loves it.*

(BILL swings back to her, grabs her in a fit of jealousy. He has to get control of himself before he can let her go)

TIM: (still 'Iago') It might even be for the best to just leave her.

BILL: I don't think I care either way.

(BILLY suddenly opens her eyes again. She starts, grabs BILL, pulls him down to her)

BILLY: Arthur!

BILL: (uncaringly) Yeah.

(She calms down immediately.)

BILLY: Arthur. The scent of the damp leaves, I think, still on your breath, I know.
  (*giggles*)
Doesn't your breath go all ticklish, though? Let's build a cellar so we can go down there. Safe and snug in the cellar. Lock the door, hinging. Arthur? Benny-Ben? Eyes in teats. Are tongues.

TIM: (quickly) Put her down there, Bill.

BILL: (thinking) It's strong enough. There's only one key.

TIM: We never even saw her. If the worse comes to the worse, we never even saw her. If he wants her, let him have her.

BILL: Who?

(TIM waves outside, obviously meaning the INTRUDER)

TIM: Him. It's better than the shotgun on us.

BILL: You said it wasn't loaded.

TIM: (sheepishly) It was loaded.
   (*then*)
Her down there, he won't even bother with us. And then what do
we know?

BILL: Nothing.

TIM: Call it Arthur and Benny-Ben.

BILL: (bitterly) Yeah.

TIM: At least we've got the knife.

BILL: What knife?

TIM: Your knife. The one you pulled out of the overcoat you had
on.

BILL: (genuinely) No overcoat. No knife.

   (*TIM goes over to lift the overcoat and search in its
   pockets. He finds the knife, but notices BILL's attention is
   diverted with BILLY for a moment and quickly replaces it
   unseen back into the pocket for possible later use*)

BILL: (straightening) Well?

TIM: (shrugs) Must have been Billy raving on about some knife I
or somebody had earlier.
   (*a quick and further denigration*)
Arthur and Ben. Would you read about it?

BILL: (nodding disgustedly) Take her feet.

   (*They lift her and carry her out to the cellar.*

   Blackout)

72

15.

(BILL and TIM return to the bedroom cautiously. They both talk in whispers. BILL creeps over to the window, looks out)

TIM: What do you think?

BILL: He might be gone.

TIM: No.

BILL: He's not going to be hanging around here all night.

TIM: (shaking head) I heard him at me.

BILL: A moment ago you weren't saying that.

TIM: (simply) It's me he's after.

BILL: Don't kid yourself.

TIM: I'm not.

BILL: So what was all your rigmarole about Billy and the cellar, then?

TIM: I need you. Not her.

BILL: With that maniac out there, we all need each other.

TIM: He's had her.

BILL: She's alive, thank God.

TIM: He has.

BILL: Look, boy, if he's after you, he's after all of us. You think about your mother over there on her own.

TIM: *I can't.*
   (*and*)
Can't you see the gun or something?

BILL: You crazy?

TIM: He can't use it.

BILL: Not unless he puts two and two together and gets into your place.

TIM: Bloody hell.

BILL: Don't worry about it. He's a knife man, remember. Read the papers. Look, you and me, we're going to get over to your place.

TIM: What about Billy?

BILL: We'll get your mother, get the ammo, get to the phone. It's a chance to take.

> (*He moves TIM towards the door. But when they reach it, instinct makes him stop and turn to the window.*
>
> *The INTRUDER's silhouette is framed there, looking in on them.*
>
> *BILL recovers first. He runs to the window, throws it open and is about to climb out when there is a deafening shot. He ducks, drops to the floor. TIM follows.*
>
> *Silence.*
>
> *Then TIM begins whimpering. In the air, too, there is the same heavy breathing, menacingly close.*

It seems to pass)

BILL: You said it wasn't loaded.

TIM: It wasn't.

BILL: That means he's been over to your place. Your mother...

TIM: What can we do?

BILL: We'll have to make it down the road.

TIM: How?

BILL: I don't know.

TIM: What about Billy?

BILL: I don't know!

(At least BILL can edge himself up in order to pull down the blind. Just as he reaches it, there is another shockingly close shot.

This time it crashes through the glass. The shock flings him across the room.

A mad laugh outside trails off.

Two more shots ring out and thud against the side of the house, harmless enough, but enough to make them dive for cover.

In a moment of terrible waiting for more, another cloud passes over the moon and plunges them into darkness.)

16.

(We hear BILL and TIM whispering through the darkness)

TIM: Where are you?

BILL: Get ready. We've got to get out of here.

TIM: *I can't.*

BILL: You've got to.

TIM: *He's all inside me.*

BILL: *Come on, you silly bastard!*

> *(The bedroom lights suddenly come back on, catching them looking very silly...)*

17.

> *(... they freeze in mid-movement of getting ready to make a dash for it, looking and feeling even more ridiculous than shocked.*
>
> *Repeated laughter from outside attests that this was no coincidence.*
>
> *At it, they drop to the floor again.*
>
> *BILL starts to edge towards the light switch, but, as if to answer his intent, the lights are switched on and off, on and off. Then stay off)*

BILL: Get ready, Tim...

> *(But at that moment the cloud passes from the moon and the*

room is flooded with moonlight once more, making them just as visible as they were when the lights were on.

Again, the laughter from outside is deliberate in its timing... as if they weren't aware how exposed they are, or aware of being toyed with)

TIM: He can see everything.

BILL: The bastard. Just don't panic.

(From down the passage, there is a violent smashing of wood. Then the sound of probably the cellar door giving way.

BILLY screams off, followed by sounds of a fierce struggle.

BILL goes to run out to help her, but is tackled and held back by TIM. The older man struggles to get free, but TIM holds on for his life)

TIM: Don't... leave....!

(BILLY screams again. Then silence.

BILL breaks past the other man, runs out down the passage.

TIM just cannot move to follow)

TIM: Help *me*!

(and huddles into himself out of abject fear.

There is a terrifying shot out by the back door. Then much scuffling noise from inside the bungalow.

BILL dashes back into the bedroom, throws himself behind the door.

BILL is now on a level of self-preservation himself)

BILL: He nearly got me.

TIM: (numbly) Billy?

BILL: Gone.

TIM: (fearing the worst) What do you mean 'gone'?

BILL: Gone, gone!

TIM: (accusatory) We should help each other. You shouldn't leave me. I know what he's after.

BILL: Piss off. I came back, didn't I? I'm pretty sure he's gone. Jesus it whistled past my ear.

TIM: He got her, didn't he?

BILL: I caught him dragging her off. Then he fired. Bloody hell!

TIM: Don't go out there again.

BILL: I haven't got the guts.

TIM: It wouldn't do you any good.

> *(BILL decides it's okay to move. He does so not to escape but to grab TIM by the neck)*

BILL: Now you start telling me what you know!

> *(But TIM is quite impervious to anything but the INTRUDER out and around and can only use BILL's nearness for more protection.*
>
> *BILL lets him go, doesn't push him away)*

BILL: Tell me now.

TIM: He's been watching. He knows all about me. I just feel him *drilling*.

BILL: (heavily) Watching, when?

TIM: (no real answer) He must have been watching when I went back to get the gun.

BILL: You said you brought it with you.

TIM: Did I?

BILL: You're still not telling me anything! How could he be doing that when he was onto Billy and me then?

TIM: I don't know! He just was.

BILL: Think again. We'll all going to start to die if you don't.
    (*TIM shakes his head, 'I can't'*)
And while you're at it, you tell me why you didn't take off back to your place to ring the police when you could have. You knew he was reported to be around here. You said you saw how we were in trouble. And how come you spout, 'I didn't do this' when we brought her in here? And how come I've got this nagging feeling it was you who king hit me. And if you don't give, I'm going to shove you out that window and you're on your own.

TIM: Don't do that!

BILL: Try me.

    (Pause)

TIM: (quietly) I might have come back after. I didn't even think of the phone. I thought... uh, I only wanted to see if you and she *would*... you know.

BILL: You telling me that was you outside watching us at first?

79

TIM: After that I left. Honestly. I didn't think of the gun. I can't remember much after that! He must have been watching me. That's what I'm trying to tell you!

BILL: (hard) You're on your own, pal.

TIM: (panicking, grabbing hold) I didn't mean to hit you so hard like that! I was joking! It's must have been how you fell, Bill!
   (*then involuntary outcry*)
She does it with everyone else! She should have let me!

   (*BILL stares at him while what TIM has said sinks in*)

BILL: Oh, God damn you!

TIM: (as though his personality has switched) You're not going to push me out there. I won't let you.

BILL: Or what?

TIM: (divertingly) It's all your fault. Why'd you keep on whispering to me about what she was... like.

BILL: Get off.

TIM: You did. You know you did. You're not going to send me out there.

BILL: When're you going to be a man?

TIM: Did you ever want me to?

BILL: (not answering that) I didn't say go and be dangerous. I didn't say anything of the sort, mate.

TIM: (almost outcry) I didn't know I was going to...

   (*He stops*)

BILL: Okay, I take a little bit of the blame. But fuck that. We've got this problem out there.

TIM: (vain hope) Do you think he's gone?

BILL: Maybe. Maybe you're right and we don't move. Maybe he's given up.

> (Long pause. As if to confirm their hope, they hear nothing but normal night sounds outside; it enhances their reflective moods)

BILL: What I was trying to say to you... and you should have realized it, or whatever... was that you get to my age thinking you can get through it without going mad. But you're wrong. Even a bit wrong is just as bad as all wrong. Like, you can sort of just call it up. I wasn't saying you should try.

TIM: I didn't.

BILL: (but with acceptance now) Yes, you did. It doesn't matter. Later it might, but not now. I was trying to go on about how you just have to scratch and there's evil just bursting to get out finally. I was trying to tell you it might be exciting, but it's sordid. You.

TIM: Me what?

BILL: I haven't felt I've lived a decent moment since.

TIM: I haven't been sorry.

BILL: Maybe not indecent, only sad.

> (TIM reaches over to touch him)

BILL: Get your hand off.

TIM: (reacting) Bugger you.

> (BILL points to outside)

BILL: Just sit there and listen to how the brute has called you up.

TIM: (but more preoccupied with:) Are we still going to say we saw nothing?

BILL: You still think we're going to get out of this?

TIM: Billy?

BILL: (utter remorse) Yes, my Billy.

TIM: (now getting the assertive one) Nothing. We didn't touch her. We didn't see her. I only came across you lying in here.

BILL: (corrective) Out there.

TIM: Out there.

BILL: You've got no hope of convincing anybody.
  (*then*)
Then again, you're young. You might be able to bluster your way through. I'll try my best for you. Just remember outside for a start.

  (*TIM now has the nerve to inch his way to the window, peeks out, sees nothing untoward. Looks back:*)

TIM: What if he doesn't...

BILL: Finish her off? You can say it. Either way, he should be coming for us. I've got no idea what's going on.
  (*then*)
Look, if he does, I'll try to hold him. You take off, go as hard as you can, no matter what you hear.

TIM: I mean, if she's still alive, she'll still think it was me going at her. Calling us Arthur and Ben, like.

BILL: (very wearily) You drop big hints I kept saying how she was just about finished when he must have got to her. Burnt out, bells in her head. She can't involve you, us, either way. Anymore.
  (*and*)
You know, she was...

> *(He stops)*

TIM: What?

BILL: I was just going to talk about importance, I guess.

TIM: Us?

> *(They just look at each other until BILL lowers his gaze. TIM goes back to peering out of the window until*
>
> *another cloud passes over the moon – and darkness)*

18.

> *(We hear their voices through the darkness:)*

BILL: What was that?

> *(At first silence follows this. Then movements inside the room)*

TIM: (hiss) What are you doing?

BILL: Looking at the sky. We've got a chance now.

TIM: I still can't.

BILL: We've got to.

*(But there is a scraping sound somewhere at hand...
certainly inside. It is obviously metal on wood.*

*Whatever it is stops. Absolute silence for a long while,
before:*

*The bedroom main light switches suddenly on and
blindingly. They both scramble towards the thin cover of
the bed.*

But nothing. Still silence.

*BILL looks carefully down the passageway, sees nothing
untoward. He goes to move over to the window but an
alarmed cry from TIM stops him by drawing his attention to
the gun barrel poking into the room, resting on the window
sill.*

*On second take, BILL notices how the gun is sitting there in
a way that clearly indicates it is not being held, but has
been left there.*

*Very cautiously BILL goes towards it. Every inch he gets
closer seems to confirm that the INTRUDER isn't 'behind'
it. He makes a grab for it.*

*In that instance, there is a cry of triumph from outside and
the blade of the knife slashes repeatedly at him through the
window.*

*He cries out, tries to ward off the blows, but is badly jabbed
about his forearms before he can react by flinging himself
backwards.*

The gun falls into the room as he does so.

There is another burst of deranged laughter from outside.

BILL has the presence of mind to go for the gun. He goes

to fire wildly at the lunatic outside but the weapon only clicks. It is quite empty.

When he realizes this, BILL drops to the floor and shouts to a witless TIM)

BILL: The lights! Get the lights!

(but has to scramble over and switch the lights off himself.

The stage is plunged into darkness again)

19.

(Through the darkness, we hear BILL trying to comfort the younger man. He himself is barely able to get his nerves under control:)

BILL: It's all right. We've got the gun, right? It's a club. It's got to be better than that knife. *The bastard.*
   (gathers himself)
We can go down and get out own knives now, right? We've got him, Timmy. We're going to be alright. We're..

(but he is cut short when:)

20.

(... a light goes on around the back. The back door opens. The kitchen light goes on. Then the lights in the living room. Then the one down the passageway.

The bland and mechanical way in which these lights are switched on is quite comparatively startling.

*Someone begins to move openly and heavily around the
kitchen, clinking glasses, opening cutlery drawers &ce, then
walks with measured steps towards the bedroom.*

*BILL and TIM brace themselves, wanting to but unable to
take any sort of initiative. All BILL can do is hold the gun
up as a sort of club, waiting fairly ineffectually for the
inevitable attack.*

*The footsteps stop outside the bedroom door. This is a
heavy moment when nobody dares to move.*

*When BILL begins to get up a little nerve to move, the
person in the passageway takes the final few steps and
stands in silhouette in the doorway.*

*The moment when BILL might have gone on the attack
passes, and the three of them realise it.*

*Finally, the INTRUDER speaks in the same psychotic voice
as earlier but with crude mockery:)*

INTRUDER: You didn't kiss each other.
   (*pauses*)
Kiss each other first.
   (*BILL and TIM don't move*)
I kissed her first. Oh, I did…
   (*pointedly*)
sir.

   (*BILL and TIM stiffen, recognizes the 'sir' parody. The
   INTRUDER, now sure of the ground anyway, just smiles
   knowingly*)

INTRUDER: I sucked her tongue… *sir.* My friend and me. Oh,
yes.

   (*When BILL still doesn't come on, the INTRUDER's tone
   rises in provocation, lewdness*)

86

INTRUDER: She called me Arthur and I said Ben. I didn't mind. I thought it was inventive, didn't we? And she whispered and I said yes. And she whispered how could I, how would I, and I said yes and yes.

(*snigger*)

Sir.

(*then*)

And she said don't and I said yes we would. And she sighed. Arthur and Ben. Oh, *sir*, didn't she sigh.

> *(BILL bellows with rage. He raises the gun and threatens to attack the INTRUDER, but when the latter evenly pulls out the knife, BILL hasn't in the final analysis got it in him to take it further.*
>
> *The INTRUDER's teeth show in a slow, knowing smile)*

INTRUDER: And you're right. She was mad. But you see... *sir*... she isn't anymore. Oh, no.

> *(Pause)*

INTRUDER: Oh, *sir*, I let her save your life. Two. Lives. Too. But then that was before she knew who was important to you, wasn't it?

> *(The INTRUDER swings his attention onto TIM obviously, and:)*

INTRUDER: Little man, leash, leash, leash, leash... and I let her save your life, too, yes, when you was behind him with the butt of that gun and coming on down on him. Yes. Would any of us ever believe she would do that?

> *(The INTRUDER leaves time for BILL to recollect that it was TIM behind him before he really got knocked out. He turns accusingly to TIM but the younger man is too terrified to deny it.*
>
> *BILL nods confirmation of the fact, lowers the gun and*

stands defenselessly)

INTRUDER: Yes, *sir*, yes.

BILL: (tonelessly) Come on then.

INTRUDER: (sickly snigger) She dies *sir*... with me rammed right up inside her giving birth. Oh, *sir*, both of us gladly.

BILL: *Come on!*

TIM: No!

> *(Incongruously, the INTRUDER begins to chuckle, however unpleasantly still. Finally:)*

INTRUDER: You think I killed her. No, *sir*, not I. Not now when I've just found her. In fact, if you look, there she is...
   (*pointing to window*)
now, *sir*.

> *(Both BILL and TIM swing around towards the window. But nobody is there.*
>
> *They turn back quickly to the doorway.*
>
> *The INTRUDER has removed the hat, and then, almost as a burlesque strip, opens and half-removes the overcoat.*
>
> *BILLY has untied her hair. It shines in the silhouette of the doorway.*
>
> *She laughs. This time it is her normal voice and it is quite startlingly gay)*

BILL: (totally nonplussed) Billy...?

BILLY: (party voice) Don't move. I've got a surprise.

> *(She slips out down the passageway. They look incapable*

of moving anyway. When she returns, she carries a bottle of liqueur and three glasses. These, she places on the floor, then pulls a chair in from the passageway to the doorway and sits on it. She reaches up and switches on the bedroom light.

She is neither blood-stained nor traumatized as she ought to be. In fact, she looks remarkably elegant in the overcoat. When she crosses her legs, it is evident she is wearing full lingerie underneath, including suspenders and stockings.

Her eyes dance at them, smiling yet flinty.

She evidently has already poured liqueur into one of the glasses, which she holds in her hand. She sips slowly from it)

BILLY: Cheers, Arthur and Benny.

BILL: (only thing to say) Are you alright?

(He goes to move towards her. She holds up her hand for him to stop right there. There is something definite in her manner which he obeys instantly.

TIM edges towards the open window)

BILLY: Oh, if I were you, I wouldn't be going, Benny boy.

(He freezes)

BILLY: I do have who is Arthur and who is Ben right, don't I?

BILL: (recovering enough) If you've got to be humoured.

BILLY: Oh, you're complaining because you were Ben? No, no, I'm sure out Timmy-wimmy was Benny-wenny. Weren't you, Tim?

(He can only look to BILL for help.

89

She laughs, drinks stylishly)

BILL: Enough of this.

(He starts forward again)

BILLY: Oh, I wouldn't move much if I was you, Arthur. You never know who's watching out there, do you?

(The possibility of this… of her being in cahoots with the real INTRUDER… stops both him and TIM again)

BILLY: Who can ever know, hmm? Besides I'm still a bit tainted, as I would be, wouldn't I?, and we wouldn't want someone getting the wrong idea it's you who're done that, no? So what I really think both of you should do is play still like lizards for a bit.
   (*then*)
Well, I would if I were you.

BILL: Is he out there?

BILLY: (sweetly) Now how would I know?

BILL: It looks like you do. What's going on?

BILLY: What's going on, Arthur asks.

BILL: Don't call me Arthur.

BILLY: You aren't really Arthur?

BILL: *Is he out there?*

BILLY: (unbothered) And he's not Ben?

TIM: (crazily) I'm Tim!

BILLY: (speaking towards the window) See, I did get it right. I've always been good at the toss of the coin.

BILL: (empty threat) I'm coming over to switch out that bloody light.

BILLY: Lordie, I wouldn't try that.
  (*then*)
But neither of you have touched your drinks.
  (*drains hers*)
The first one who dares, pours for me too.
  (*neither man moves*)
You did ask me to go out and bring you drinkies, didn't you?

BILL: Bullshit to this.

BILLY: Bullshit to what?

BILL: Bullshit.

> *(He forces himself to go over to the window but is very cautious in looking out. Of course he doesn't see anyone out there, although he doesn't try too hard.*
>
> *To keep her advantage, she commands:)*

BILLY: Say you did, Arthur.

BILL: (with grit) I'm Bill, you dope.

BILLY: (at TIM) Say you did, Bensy.

> *(TIM is totally confused now and BILL can't or won't help)*

BILLY: (helping him out) That you asked me to pop out and get the drinks.

TIM: Yes.

BILLY: Yes what?

TIM: I asked you to go out and bring back the drinks.

BILLY: No, that's not right.
  (*then very menacingly*)
Whisper it, you little shit.

TIM: (quickly doing so) I asked you to get some drinks.

BILLY: (no mean threat) Lay on the bed and say it right.

  (*TIM doesn't hesitate in lying on the bed to:*)

TIM: I asked you if you'd mind getting a few drinks.

  (*In this meantime, BILL has determined there is no threat, at least immediately. He goes over, picks up bottle and glass*)

BILL: Well, I could use one.

  (*She holds out her own glass for refill*)

BILLY: (no beg-your-pardons) Don't forget me.

BILL: (mumble) No.

BILLY: No, you'd never do that, would Arthur?
  (*and when he doesn't:*)
I should move well away now, shouldn't you?

  (*He means to leave the room, but her chair is blocking the doorway*)

BILL: You're blocking the door.

BILLY: I am, aren't we?

  (*This is a battle of wits. He finally gives up, turns back into the room*)

BILLY: Such a pity this foul Irish muck was all I could find. We really should have had some champers on ice, you know, Arthur.

(She kicks over the bottle and the glasses from where she sits, and does so towards them. They are like attempts at physical assault)

BILLY: Is that the gun my friend was supposed to be using?

BILL: Is that nutcase still out there?

TIM: (answering for her) *Of course he is.*

BILLY: (ignoring that) Good Lord, would you call him a nutcase to his face?

(He doesn't answer, just in case.

She smiles away to TIM, indicates gun)

BILLY: Is that absurd thing still not loaded, Ben? If my friend and I point it right into your face, will it just click, do you think?

(TIM is both too guilty and too cowered to answer)

BILL: (an appeal) Where is he, Billy?

(She just smiles back blankly. It gives BILL encouragement to be bolder now that no actual threat has materialized. He goes to the window again, not outright boldly but at least as casually as he can.

There he looks out more exactly than before. Still, he sees nothing.

He turns back to her)

BILL: Nobody's out there, is there?

BILLY: (smiling tauntingly) No?

BILL: (bet hedging) Let's all take it easy, okay?
  (*indicates bottle and glasses*)
Why don't we take these into the living room?

BILLY: Give time for that brute of yours to slink back into the black hole at the centre of your life? That sort of thing?

> *(This stops him on it being a recollection of what he said to TIM)*

BILLY: Well, something like that, no? You said it, I didn't.

> *(BILL takes up a glass, pours himself a drink. Hands half of it to TIM.*
>
> *She watches with amusement how TIM has trouble swallowing it down)*

BILLY: If our Ben here has trouble getting that down, can we be sure he'll remember if the gun is loaded or not?

BILL: Let's start with our real names, shall we?

BILLY: Oh? Have I got it all wrong again?

BILL: You're been through the ringer, that's all.

BILLY: Have I?

BILL: You have. You mightn't be able to remember half of it, thank God.

BILLY: I just wanted to have a little look at it.

BILL: What?

BILLY: The gun Ben's so fascinated with.

94

(She holds out her hand for it. BILL hesitates, then goes to take the gun. TIM grabs it as the only protection he has. They have a small tug-of-war over it, before BILL wins, and, very reluctantly, hands it to her)

BILLY: Oh no, Arthur. I wanted Ben to bring it over. Please, pretty pussy please...?

(BILL thrusts it into TIM's hands, motions to humour her. The younger man very warily takes it over to her.

She takes it calmly; only examines it a little as though it was a vaguely amusing little toy before she cradles it and settles back into her chair)

BILLY: Ah well, boys, it's been a long night, wouldn't we say? But flakes of memory, right? All dropping away. Sloughing off, sort of. Do you think that might be what keeps families together, that sloughing off? Or is it picking up the flakes? Gosh gee, I don't know. We should have breakfast, too. Bacon laid on thick. Sizzling good old red bloody meat. Like the sun I really want to see coming up, don't you?
(then directly at him)
See, you're absolutely right, Arthur. I can talk about it now, those bits of memory. In a lizard's tongue kind of way. So shall we all start wagging out fork tongues so all our friends can hear?

(BILL and TIM have begun to relax)

BILL: He's not out there, is he?

BILLY: ('don't know', but still:) Oh, I wouldn't have thought so. But who knows?

BILL: Jesus, when I saw you dragged off I thought...

BILLY: Oh, *that*. That was just the wheat bag really. Isn't it funny how people who go around saying people are mad turn out to be imagining things themselves.

95

(The other two are very much on guard again, but it comes out rather comically)

TIM: That wasn't the wheat bag!

BILL: What do you mean the wheat bag?

BILLY: Let's not spoil our quiet drinkies over some old wheat bag, Arthur and Ben.
  (toasts)
Here's to this morning.

BILL: Yeah.

BILLY: (at TIM) Here's to this morning.

BILL: Yeah.

BILLY: (at TIM) Here's to this morning.

BILL: Yeah.

BILLY: (at TIM) You're not toasting this morning, Benny boy? I think you ought to.

TIM: This morning.

(As they drink, BILLY puts down her glass, casually pulls two shot cartridges from the pocket of the raincoat, and loads the gun)

BILLY: You were right. It wasn't loaded. How clever you are, Ben.

BILL: Enough, Billy.

BILLY: I used to be a very good shot, didn't I? My friend tells me it's easier with a shotgun. Would that be right?

(They freeze when she slowly brings the gun up to aim at

96

*them. Her voice takes on an edge now while keeping its
mocking tone)*

BILLY: Well, my Arthur and Ben, you two have had a grand old
time together, eh?

BILL: It's been a nightmare.

TIM: She doesn't mean that.

BILL: Of course I don't mean that, Ben. But when I was running
around outside like that old harpy of yours I got to thinking,
honestly what's a gal coming to? Do you know what I mean? I'm
sure you do. Popping off this silly old gun. Switching the lights
on and off. Talk about funny old games. Quite fun, really.
(drops her amusement; to BILL)
Just a teeny-weeny assistance from my own brute, my dear. Not
much. But enough. So I know what you meant about your own
life.

(BILL goes to move towards her)

BILLY: Sit on the bed, lovey.

*(with the gun pointed directly at him, he does so. She
motions the barrel at TIM in a clear meaning he should join
BILL on the bed. He does so quickly)*

BILLY: I rather enjoyed tonight. Making new friends and all
that. Just the thing for getting over feeling to be a bit of the wet
rag really. Oh, and not forgetting how tonight you made me
remember how beautiful it was with my Arthur and my Ben.
Fancy me saying their names aloud when I was in hospital and you
hearing! You tell me the odds on that! Oh, we had a fine old
time.

BILL: You don't want the gun, Billy.

BILLY: But you two have just given it to me, dear. And, yes,
you know who I think my Arthur and Ben were? If I remember

97

rightly they were some neighbour's pets when I was knee high to a grasshopper. And apparently one day I went and gave them a drinkies out of an old tin of arsenic like you had in those days.

(*and*)

Just like one of your drinks there.

(They put down their drinks quickly)

BILLY: Poor little things, though they looked big and nasty to me then, I think.

BILL: (meaning the drinks) Which one?

BILLY: Arthur or Ben? Now you know I can't remember which was Arthur and which was Ben. I supposed it must have been the one who really *meant* me the most harm. I guess only you two would know that, no? All I remember one they shot one but it turns out to be the wrong one. It was the other that had the poison, but I still can't remember if that was Arthur or Ben.

(*then*)

Of course, it could be what my friend said. That I'd made it all up.

TIM: (whine) *You've always been after me.*

BILLY: Of course I have, Ben. You've always been so pretty.

TIM: *You should leave me alone!*

BILLY: Why? I enjoyed so much seeing you squirm.

(Almost in triumphant justification of his terrorizing of her, he turns to BILL and:)

TIM: There, she…

(She shoots him.

It is quite unemotionally, almost as a matter of fact.

Nor does her gun waver when she turns it on TIM)

BILL: Billy, my head isn't feeling the best. I got hit hard.

BILLY: Oh? So what do you want, a kiss-off? Have you made a choice on that too?
  (he nods quickly)
But what makes you think there's any choices left for either of us to take?

> *(As if to answer, a brick is thrown crashingly into the room through the window.*
>
> *BILL jumps in shock.*
>
> *BILLY puts the gun down, pushes it well away from her with her foot. She shrugs)*

BILLY: It's just one of our bricks. Appropriate, really. He said he was a builder at heart. And he asked me so nice and politely if he could have a loan of it. I hope you don't mind that I said yes, but I'm not too sure I said to return it through the window.

BILL: (in fright, realisation) Is he leaving now?

BILLY: I don't think so.

BILL: (indicating gun) Have you got any more shells?

BILLY: He only gave me one. The choice was mine.

BILL: You could have got him.
  (*answers himself*)
No, you didn't want to, did you.

BILLY: (truly so) Are you scared? I am. I am.

> *(She gets up and goes over to him having well and truly come down from her high. On the bed, she grips him hard)*

BILLY: (barely able to speak) It's frightening.

(There is a meaningful and very close movement outside the window)

BILL: Is he mad?

BILLY: (deadpan) Yes.

BILL: Is he dead mad?

BILLY: Yes.

BILL: Real dead mad?

BILLY: Yes.

(Blackout)

(End)